OUR ADVENTURE BOOK

THIS BUCKET LIST IS THE CREATION OF

AND

IF FOUND, PLEASE CONTACT US URGENTLY:

📞

✉

THE MASTER LIST

PAGE	ACTIVITY	DONE
1		
2		
3		
4		
5		
6		
7		
8		
9		
10		
11		
12		
13		
14		
15		
16		
17		
18		
19		
20		
21		
22		
23		
24		
25		

PAGE	ACTIVITY	DONE
26		
27		
28		
29		
30		
31		
32		
33		
34		
35		
36		
37		
38		
39		
40		
41		
42		
43		
44		
45		
46		
47		
48		
49		
50		

THE MASTER LIST

PAGE	ACTIVITY	DONE
51		
52		
53		
54		
55		
56		
57		
58		
59		
60		
61		
62		
63		
64		
65		
66		
67		
68		
69		
70		
71		
72		
73		
74		
75		

PAGE	ACTIVITY	DONE
76		
77		
78		
79		
80		
81		
82		
83		
84		
85		
86		
87		
88		
89		
90		
91		
92		
93		
94		
95		
96		
97		
98		
99		
100		

IDEA TRIGGERS

ACCOLADE
ACCOMPLISH
ACCUMULATE
ACQUIRE
ACT
ACTUALIZE
AD-LIB
ADVANCE
ADVENTURE
AFFECT CHANGE
AGGREGATE
ALLURING
AMASS
AMBROSIAL
AMEND
AMUSEMENT
ANNIVERSARY
APPEALING
APPEARANCE
AROUSE
ASSOCIATE
ATHLETICS
ATTAIN
AVANT GARDE
BETTER
BIKING
BIZARRE
BLESS
BOLD
BOOST
BREAKTHROUGH
BRING ABOUT
BUILD
BURROW
BUSINESS
CALL UP
CAPER
CAPTIVATING
CAPTURE
CAROUSE
CAUSE
CELEBRATION
CEREMONY
CHANCE
CHARMING
CHOOSE
CIRCUMSTANCE
CLEANSE
CLUSTER
COINCIDENCE
COLLECT
COLORFUL
COME UP WITH
COME-HITHER
COMPLETE
COMPOSE
CONCEIVE
CONCENTRATE
CONCLUDE
CONCOCT
CONGREGATE

CONSECRATE
CONSTRUCT
CONTINGENCY
CONVERGE
COOK UP
COURAGEOUS
CREATE
CROWD
CRUISING
CULTIVATE
CURIOUS
CUTE
DALLIANCE
DAUNTLESS
DECISION
DECORATION
DEDICATE
DEED
DELECTABLE
DELICIOUAS
DELIGHT
DELIGHTFUL
DELIVER
DELVE INTO
DESIGN
DESIROUS
DEVELOP
DEVISE
DIFFERENT
DIG INTO
DISCOVER
DISCOVERY
DISHY
DISPORT
DISPOSED
DISTINCTION
DISTRACTION
DIVERSION
DO
DONATION
DREAM UP
DREAMY
DRINK TO
DRIVE
EAGER
EARN WINGS
EFFECT
ELATE
ELEVATE
EMBOLDEN
ENACT
ENDOWMENT
ENERGIZE
ENHANCE
ENKINDLE
ENLIVEN
ENTERPRISE
ENTICING
ENVISION
ESTABLISH
EVENING

EVENT
EXALT
EXAMINE
EXCITE
EXCLUSIVE
EXCURSION
EXHILARATE
EXPEDITION
EXPERIENCE
EXTERNAL
EXTRAORDINARY
FAR OUT
FASCINATING
FASHION
FATHER
FEARLESS
FEAST
FEAT
FEATHER IN CAP
FESTIVITY
FETCHING
FIND
FINISH
FIRE UP

GLOBE-TROTTING
GLORIFY
GO INTO
GOLD STAR
GROUND
GROUP
HALLOW
HANG AROUND
HANG OUT
HAPPENING
HAPPINESS
HARDY
HATCH
HAVE A BALL
HAVE A LOOK
HEAP
HEARTEN
HEAVENLY
HELP
HEROIC
HOLIDAY
HONOR
HOP
HOT

JOKE
JOKING
JUBILATE
JUNKET
KEEP
KICK UP HEELS
KINKY
KISSABLE
LAND
LANDMARK
LARK
LAUD
LAY FOUNDATION
LEAP
LET LOOSE
LIBIDINOUS
LINE
LIVE
LIVE IT UP
LODGE
LONG SHOT
LOOK INTO
LOOK UP
LOTTERY

OBSERVE
OBTAIN
OCCASION
OCCUPATION
OCCURRENCE
OFF-THE-CUFF
ONE AND ONLY
OPPORTUNITY
ORDER
ORGANIZE
ORIGINATE
OUTLANDISH
OUTSIDE CHANCE
OVERHAUL
OVERNIGHT
PAINT TOWN RED
PARENT
PARTY
PASS
PASSAGE
PASTIME
PATCH UP
PAUSE
PERFECT

PROSPECT
PROVIDE
PROVOCATIVE
PROVOKING
PUBLICIZE
PUNCH
PURIFY
PURSUIT
PUT
QUICKEN
QUIET
RACK UP
RACY
RAFFLE
RAISE
RAISE HELL
RALLY
RAMBLE
RARE
REACH
REACTIVATE
READY
REALIZE
REASSEMBLE

REUNIFY
REUNITE
REVAMP
REVEL
REVERE
REVISE
REVITALIZE
REVIVE
RIDE
RIDING
RING IN
RISK
RISQUÉ
ROMANTIC
ROMP
ROUND UP
ROUSE
SABBATICAL
SAILING
SCARE
SCENE
SCHEME
SCHOLARSHIP
SCOPE
SCORE
SCOUT
SEAFARING
SEAL
SEARCH
SECURE
SEDUCTIVE
SEEK
SENSUAL
SET DOWN
SET IN MOTION
SET RIGHT
SET UP
SETTLE
SEXY
SHAPE UP
SHARPEN
SHIFT
SHOT IN THE DARK
SIGHTSEEING
SIGN
SIRE
SITUATION
SKYROCKET
SOJOURN
SOLVE
SPARE MOMENTS
SPARE TIME
SPARK
SPAWN
SPEC
SPECULATION
SPICY
SPIRITED
SPORT
SPORTS
SPRUCE

SPRUCE UP
SPUNKY
SPUR
STABILIZE
STACK UP
START
START BALL
ROLLING
START OFF
STATION
STAY
STEAMY
STIMULATE
STOCKPILE
STOPOVER
STORY
STRAIGHTEN OUT
STRANGE
STRIKE
STRIKING
SUAVE
SUGGESTIVE
SWARM
SWING
TAKE OFF
TEASING
TEST
THING
THRONG
THROW DICE
TIME OFF
TITILLATING
TOUCH
TOUR
TRANSIT
TRAVEL
TRAVERSE
TREKKING
TRIP
TRIUMPH
TROPHY
TRY
TURN ON
TURNING POINT
UNAFRAID
UNCOMMON
UNDERTAKING
UNFAMILIAR
UNFLINCHING
UNITE
UNUSUAL
UP FOR
UPGRADE
VACATION
VALIANT
VALOROUS
VENTURE
VOYAGE
WAGER
WALK
WANDER

STUCK FOR INSPIRATION? CLOSE YOUR EYES AND PLACE A DOT AT RANDOM. COME UP WITH A CHALLENGE BASED ON THE CLOSEST WORD.

FIX
FLING
FLIRTATIOUS
FLOCK
FLYING
FOLLOW THROUGH
FOOLERY
FOREIGN
FORGE
FORM
FORMULATE
FRAME
FREEDOM
FRISK
FROLIC
FULFILL
FUN
GAIN
GAIN GROUND
GALLANT
GALVANIZE
GAME
GAMING
GENERATE
GET
GET DONE
GET TOGETHER
GIFT
GIVE LIFE TO
GLAMOROUS

HUDDLE
HUMOR
HUNT
IMAGINE
IMPRESS
IMPROVE
IMPROVISE
INCIDENT
INCLINED
INCREASE
INDIVIDUAL
INFLUENCE
INFORM
INFUSE
INITIATE
INQUISITIVE
INSPECT
INSPIRIT
INSTALL
INSTILL
INSTITUTE
INTERESTED
INTREPID
INTRODUCED
INVENT
INVEST
INVIGORATE
INVITE
JEST
JOIN

LUSCIOUS
MAKE
MAKE MERRY
MAKE OVER
MAKE STRIDES
MAKE THE SCENE
MAKE UP
MAKE WHOOPEE
MANAGE
MARVEL
MASS
MATCH
MATTER
MEET
MEET AGAIN
MEMORIALIZE
MEND
MERRIMENT
MERRYMAKING
MILESTONE
MIRACLE
MOBILIZE
MOOR
MOTIVATE
MOVE
MOVEMENT
MUSTER
NAVIGATION
NEGOTIATE
NERVY

PERFORM
PERK UP
PERSEVERING
PERSISTENT
PHASE
PHENOMENON
PICK UP
PILE UP
PLACE
PLAN
PLAY
PLEASING
PLEASURE
PLUCK
PLUCKY
POKE
POLISH
PRACTICE
PRAISE
PRANK
PRECIOUS
PREPARED
PROCLAIM
PROCREATE
PRODUCE
PROGRESS
PROJECT
PROMOTE
PROMPT
PROPEL

REASSURE
RECESS
RECONCILE
RECONDITION
RECONVENE
RECOVER
RECREATE
RECREATION
RECTIFY
RECUPERATE
REFINE
REFORM
REFRESH
REFURBISH
REJOICE
REJOIN
REKINDLE
RELAXATION
REMAKE
REMODEL
RENEW
REPAIR
RESEARCH
RESOLUTE
RESOLVE
REST
RESTORE
RESURRECT
RETIREMENT
RETRIEVE

THIS WOULD BE PERFECT FOR US BECAUSE...

_____

_____

_____

_____

MAKE IT HAPPEN: HOW? WHEN?

_____

_____

_____

_____

_____

REVIEW

DATE COMPLETED: / /

WHAT HAPPENED? (PEOPLE MET, HIGH POINTS, CHALLENGES, EXPECTATIONS VS REALITY)

_____

_____

_____

_____

THE BEST PART WAS...

_____

_____

_____

_____

_____

BUDGET

$ _____

ANTICIPATED DATE

/ /   TO   / /

ACTION LIST

⊘ _____
⊘ _____
⊘ _____
⊘ _____
⊘ _____
⊘ _____
⊘ _____
⊘ _____
⊘ _____

SUCCESS!

PLACE A CHECK HERE TO
TAKE IT OFF YOUR BUCKET LIST

RATE THIS ACTIVITY

☆☆☆☆☆

THIS WOULD BE PERFECT FOR US BECAUSE...

_____

_____

_____

MAKE IT HAPPEN: HOW? WHEN?

_____

_____

_____

_____

REVIEW

DATE COMPLETED: / /

WHAT HAPPENED? (PEOPLE MET, HIGH POINTS, CHALLENGES, EXPECTATIONS VS REALITY)

_____

_____

_____

_____

THE BEST PART WAS...

_____

_____

_____

_____

BUDGET

$

ANTICIPATED DATE

/ /   TO   / /

ACTION LIST

⊘ _____
⊘ _____
⊘ _____
⊘ _____
⊘ _____
⊘ _____
⊘ _____
⊘ _____
⊘ _____

SUCCESS!

PLACE A CHECK HERE TO
TAKE IT OFF YOUR BUCKET LIST

RATE THIS ACTIVITY

☆☆☆☆☆

ITEM #3: _____

THIS WOULD BE PERFECT FOR US BECAUSE...

_____

_____

_____

MAKE IT HAPPEN: HOW? WHEN?

_____

_____

_____

_____

_____

REVIEW

DATE COMPLETED: / /

WHAT HAPPENED? (PEOPLE MET, HIGH POINTS, CHALLENGES, EXPECTATIONS VS REALITY)

_____

_____

_____

_____

THE BEST PART WAS...

_____

_____

_____

_____

_____

BUDGET

$ _____

ANTICIPATED DATE

/ /   TO   / /

ACTION LIST

⊘ _____
⊘ _____
⊘ _____
⊘ _____
⊘ _____
⊘ _____
⊘ _____
⊘ _____
⊘ _____

SUCCESS!

PLACE A CHECK HERE TO
TAKE IT OFF YOUR BUCKET LIST

RATE THIS ACTIVITY

☆☆☆☆☆

PRIORITY ☆☆☆☆☆   ITEM #4: _____

THIS WOULD BE PERFECT FOR US BECAUSE...
_____
_____
_____

MAKE IT HAPPEN: HOW? WHEN?
_____
_____
_____
_____
_____

REVIEW
DATE COMPLETED: / /

WHAT HAPPENED? (PEOPLE MET, HIGH POINTS, CHALLENGES, EXPECTATIONS VS REALITY)
_____
_____
_____

THE BEST PART WAS...
_____
_____
_____
_____

BUDGET

$

ANTICIPATED DATE

/ /   TO   / /

ACTION LIST
⊘ _____
⊘ _____
⊘ _____
⊘ _____
⊘ _____
⊘ _____
⊘ _____
⊘ _____
⊘ _____

SUCCESS!

PLACE A CHECK HERE TO
TAKE IT OFF YOUR BUCKET LIST

RATE THIS ACTIVITY
☆☆☆☆☆

THIS WOULD BE PERFECT FOR US BECAUSE...

_____

_____

_____

_____

MAKE IT HAPPEN: HOW? WHEN?

_____

_____

_____

_____

_____

REVIEW

DATE COMPLETED: / /

WHAT HAPPENED? (PEOPLE MET, HIGH POINTS, CHALLENGES, EXPECTATIONS VS REALITY)

_____

_____

_____

_____

THE BEST PART WAS...

_____

_____

_____

_____

_____

BUDGET

$

_____

ANTICIPATED DATE

/ /   TO   / /

_____

ACTION LIST

⊘ _____

⊘ _____

⊘ _____

⊘ _____

⊘ _____

⊘ _____

⊘ _____

⊘ _____

⊘ _____

SUCCESS!

PLACE A CHECK HERE TO
TAKE IT OFF YOUR BUCKET LIST

RATE THIS ACTIVITY

☆☆☆☆☆

THIS WOULD BE PERFECT FOR US BECAUSE...

_____
_____
_____
_____

MAKE IT HAPPEN: HOW? WHEN?

_____
_____
_____
_____
_____

REVIEW

DATE COMPLETED: / /

WHAT HAPPENED? (PEOPLE MET, HIGH POINTS, CHALLENGES, EXPECTATIONS VS REALITY)

_____
_____
_____
_____

THE BEST PART WAS...

_____
_____
_____
_____

BUDGET

$

ANTICIPATED DATE

/ /   TO   / /

ACTION LIST

- ⊘ _____
- ⊘ _____
- ⊘ _____
- ⊘ _____
- ⊘ _____
- ⊘ _____
- ⊘ _____
- ⊘ _____
- ⊘ _____

SUCCESS!

PLACE A CHECK HERE TO
TAKE IT OFF YOUR BUCKET LIST

RATE THIS ACTIVITY

☆☆☆☆☆

THIS WOULD BE PERFECT FOR US BECAUSE...

BUDGET

$

ANTICIPATED DATE

/ /   TO   / /

MAKE IT HAPPEN: HOW? WHEN?

ACTION LIST

⊘ _____
⊘ _____
⊘ _____
⊘ _____
⊘ _____
⊘ _____
⊘ _____
⊘ _____
⊘ _____

REVIEW

DATE COMPLETED: / /

WHAT HAPPENED? (PEOPLE MET, HIGH POINTS, CHALLENGES, EXPECTATIONS VS REALITY)

SUCCESS!

PLACE A CHECK HERE TO
TAKE IT OFF YOUR BUCKET LIST

RATE THIS ACTIVITY

☆☆☆☆☆

THE BEST PART WAS...

I'VE MISSED MORE THAN 9000 SHOTS IN MY CAREER. I'VE LOST ALMOST 300 GAMES. 26 TIMES I'VE BEEN TRUSTED TO TAKE THE GAME WINNING SHOT AND MISSED. I'VE FAILED OVER AND OVER AND OVER AGAIN IN MY LIFE. AND THAT IS WHY I SUCCEED. – MICHAEL JORDAN

THIS WOULD BE PERFECT FOR US BECAUSE...

_____

_____

_____

MAKE IT HAPPEN: HOW? WHEN?

_____

_____

_____

_____

_____

_____

REVIEW

DATE COMPLETED: / /

WHAT HAPPENED? (PEOPLE MET, HIGH POINTS, CHALLENGES, EXPECTATIONS VS REALITY)

_____

_____

_____

_____

_____

THE BEST PART WAS...

_____

_____

_____

_____

_____

BUDGET

$

ANTICIPATED DATE

/ /   TO   / /

ACTION LIST

⊘ _____
⊘ _____
⊘ _____
⊘ _____
⊘ _____
⊘ _____
⊘ _____
⊘ _____
⊘ _____

SUCCESS!

PLACE A CHECK HERE TO
TAKE IT OFF YOUR BUCKET LIST

RATE THIS ACTIVITY

☆☆☆☆☆

THE MOST DIFFICULT THING IS THE DECISION TO ACT, THE REST IS MERELY TENACITY. — AMELIA EARHART

THIS WOULD BE PERFECT FOR US BECAUSE...

_____
_____
_____

MAKE IT HAPPEN: HOW? WHEN?

_____
_____
_____
_____

REVIEW

DATE COMPLETED: / /

WHAT HAPPENED? (PEOPLE MET, HIGH POINTS, CHALLENGES, EXPECTATIONS VS REALITY)

_____
_____
_____
_____

THE BEST PART WAS...

_____
_____
_____
_____
_____

BUDGET

$ _____

ANTICIPATED DATE

/ /   TO   / /

ACTION LIST

⊘ _____
⊘ _____
⊘ _____
⊘ _____
⊘ _____
⊘ _____
⊘ _____
⊘ _____
⊘ _____

SUCCESS!

PLACE A CHECK HERE TO
TAKE IT OFF YOUR BUCKET LIST

RATE THIS ACTIVITY

☆☆☆☆☆

THIS WOULD BE PERFECT FOR US BECAUSE...

BUDGET

$

ANTICIPATED DATE

/ /   TO   / /

MAKE IT HAPPEN: HOW? WHEN?

ACTION LIST

⊘ _____
⊘ _____
⊘ _____
⊘ _____
⊘ _____
⊘ _____
⊘ _____
⊘ _____
⊘ _____

REVIEW

DATE COMPLETED: / /

WHAT HAPPENED? (PEOPLE MET, HIGH POINTS, CHALLENGES, EXPECTATIONS VS REALITY)

SUCCESS!

PLACE A CHECK HERE TO
TAKE IT OFF YOUR BUCKET LIST

THE BEST PART WAS...

RATE THIS ACTIVITY

☆☆☆☆☆

ITEM #11: _____

THIS WOULD BE PERFECT FOR US BECAUSE...

_____
_____
_____

MAKE IT HAPPEN: HOW? WHEN?

_____
_____
_____
_____
_____

REVIEW

DATE COMPLETED: / /

WHAT HAPPENED? (PEOPLE MET, HIGH POINTS, CHALLENGES, EXPECTATIONS VS REALITY)

_____
_____
_____
_____

THE BEST PART WAS...

_____
_____
_____
_____
_____

BUDGET

$ _____

ANTICIPATED DATE

/ / TO / /

ACTION LIST

⊘ _____
⊘ _____
⊘ _____
⊘ _____
⊘ _____
⊘ _____
⊘ _____
⊘ _____
⊘ _____

SUCCESS!

PLACE A CHECK HERE TO
TAKE IT OFF YOUR BUCKET LIST

RATE THIS ACTIVITY

☆☆☆☆☆

THIS WOULD BE PERFECT FOR US BECAUSE...

BUDGET

$

ANTICIPATED DATE

/ /   TO   / /

MAKE IT HAPPEN: HOW? WHEN?

ACTION LIST

⊘ _____
⊘ _____
⊘ _____
⊘ _____
⊘ _____
⊘ _____
⊘ _____
⊘ _____
⊘ _____

REVIEW

DATE COMPLETED: / /

SUCCESS!

WHAT HAPPENED? (PEOPLE MET, HIGH POINTS, CHALLENGES, EXPECTATIONS VS REALITY)

PLACE A CHECK HERE TO
TAKE IT OFF YOUR BUCKET LIST

RATE THIS ACTIVITY

☆☆☆☆☆

THE BEST PART WAS...

THIS WOULD BE PERFECT FOR US BECAUSE...

_____
_____
_____
_____

MAKE IT HAPPEN: HOW? WHEN?

_____
_____
_____
_____
_____

REVIEW

DATE COMPLETED: / /

WHAT HAPPENED? (PEOPLE MET, HIGH POINTS, CHALLENGES, EXPECTATIONS VS REALITY)

_____
_____
_____
_____

THE BEST PART WAS...

_____
_____
_____
_____
_____

BUDGET

$ _____

ANTICIPATED DATE

/ /   TO   / /

ACTION LIST

- ⊘ _____
- ⊘ _____
- ⊘ _____
- ⊘ _____
- ⊘ _____
- ⊘ _____
- ⊘ _____
- ⊘ _____
- ⊘ _____

SUCCESS!

PLACE A CHECK HERE TO
TAKE IT OFF YOUR BUCKET LIST

RATE THIS ACTIVITY

☆☆☆☆☆

THIS WOULD BE PERFECT FOR US BECAUSE...

BUDGET

$

ANTICIPATED DATE

/ /   TO   / /

MAKE IT HAPPEN: HOW? WHEN?

ACTION LIST

⊘
⊘
⊘
⊘
⊘
⊘
⊘
⊘
⊘

REVIEW

DATE COMPLETED: / /

WHAT HAPPENED? (PEOPLE MET, HIGH POINTS, CHALLENGES, EXPECTATIONS VS REALITY)

SUCCESS!

THE BEST PART WAS...

PLACE A CHECK HERE TO
TAKE IT OFF YOUR BUCKET LIST

RATE THIS ACTIVITY

☆☆☆☆☆

TWENTY YEARS FROM NOW YOU WILL BE MORE DISAPPOINTED BY THE THINGS
THAT YOU DIDN'T DO THAN BY THE ONES YOU DID DO. — MARK TWAIN

THIS WOULD BE PERFECT FOR US BECAUSE...

MAKE IT HAPPEN: HOW? WHEN?

REVIEW

DATE COMPLETED: / /

WHAT HAPPENED? (PEOPLE MET, HIGH POINTS, CHALLENGES, EXPECTATIONS VS REALITY)

THE BEST PART WAS...

BUDGET

$

ANTICIPATED DATE

/ /   TO   / /

ACTION LIST

⊘ _____
⊘ _____
⊘ _____
⊘ _____
⊘ _____
⊘ _____
⊘ _____
⊘ _____
⊘ _____

SUCCESS!

PLACE A CHECK HERE TO
TAKE IT OFF YOUR BUCKET LIST

RATE THIS ACTIVITY

☆☆☆☆☆

THIS WOULD BE PERFECT FOR US BECAUSE...

MAKE IT HAPPEN: HOW? WHEN?

REVIEW

DATE COMPLETED: /   /

WHAT HAPPENED? (PEOPLE MET, HIGH POINTS, CHALLENGES, EXPECTATIONS VS REALITY)

THE BEST PART WAS...

BUDGET

$

ANTICIPATED DATE

/ /   TO   / /

ACTION LIST

⊘ _____
⊘ _____
⊘ _____
⊘ _____
⊘ _____
⊘ _____
⊘ _____
⊘ _____
⊘ _____

SUCCESS!

PLACE A CHECK HERE TO
TAKE IT OFF YOUR BUCKET LIST

RATE THIS ACTIVITY

☆☆☆☆☆

THIS WOULD BE PERFECT FOR US BECAUSE...

_____
_____
_____
_____

MAKE IT HAPPEN: HOW? WHEN?

_____
_____
_____
_____
_____

REVIEW

DATE COMPLETED: / /

WHAT HAPPENED? (PEOPLE MET, HIGH POINTS, CHALLENGES, EXPECTATIONS VS REALITY)

_____
_____
_____
_____

THE BEST PART WAS...

_____
_____
_____
_____
_____

BUDGET

$

ANTICIPATED DATE

/ /   TO   / /

ACTION LIST

- ⊘ _____
- ⊘ _____
- ⊘ _____
- ⊘ _____
- ⊘ _____
- ⊘ _____
- ⊘ _____
- ⊘ _____
- ⊘ _____

SUCCESS!

PLACE A CHECK HERE TO
TAKE IT OFF YOUR BUCKET LIST

RATE THIS ACTIVITY

☆☆☆☆☆

THIS WOULD BE PERFECT FOR US BECAUSE...

MAKE IT HAPPEN: HOW? WHEN?

REVIEW

DATE COMPLETED: / /

WHAT HAPPENED? (PEOPLE MET, HIGH POINTS, CHALLENGES, EXPECTATIONS VS REALITY)

THE BEST PART WAS...

BUDGET

$

ANTICIPATED DATE

/ /   TO   / /

ACTION LIST

⊘ _____
⊘ _____
⊘ _____
⊘ _____
⊘ _____
⊘ _____
⊘ _____
⊘ _____
⊘ _____

SUCCESS!

PLACE A CHECK HERE TO
TAKE IT OFF YOUR BUCKET LIST

RATE THIS ACTIVITY

☆☆☆☆☆

THE BEST TIME TO PLANT A TREE WAS 20 YEARS AGO... THE SECOND BEST TIME IS NOW. – CHINESE PROVERB

THIS WOULD BE PERFECT FOR US BECAUSE...

_____

_____

_____

MAKE IT HAPPEN: HOW? WHEN?

_____

_____

_____

_____

REVIEW

DATE COMPLETED: / /

WHAT HAPPENED? (PEOPLE MET, HIGH POINTS, CHALLENGES, EXPECTATIONS VS REALITY)

_____

_____

_____

_____

THE BEST PART WAS...

_____

_____

_____

_____

BUDGET

$ _____

ANTICIPATED DATE

/ /　TO　/ /

ACTION LIST

⊘ _____
⊘ _____
⊘ _____
⊘ _____
⊘ _____
⊘ _____
⊘ _____
⊘ _____
⊘ _____

SUCCESS!

PLACE A CHECK HERE TO
TAKE IT OFF YOUR BUCKET LIST

RATE THIS ACTIVITY

☆☆☆☆☆

THIS WOULD BE PERFECT FOR US BECAUSE...

MAKE IT HAPPEN: HOW? WHEN?

REVIEW

DATE COMPLETED: / /

WHAT HAPPENED? (PEOPLE MET, HIGH POINTS, CHALLENGES, EXPECTATIONS VS REALITY)

THE BEST PART WAS...

BUDGET

$

ANTICIPATED DATE

/ /   TO   / /

ACTION LIST

⊘ _____
⊘ _____
⊘ _____
⊘ _____
⊘ _____
⊘ _____
⊘ _____
⊘ _____
⊘ _____

SUCCESS!

PLACE A CHECK HERE TO
TAKE IT OFF YOUR BUCKET LIST

RATE THIS ACTIVITY

☆☆☆☆☆

THIS WOULD BE PERFECT FOR US BECAUSE...

_____

_____

_____

MAKE IT HAPPEN: HOW? WHEN?

_____

_____

_____

_____

REVIEW

DATE COMPLETED: / /

WHAT HAPPENED? (PEOPLE MET, HIGH POINTS, CHALLENGES, EXPECTATIONS VS REALITY)

_____

_____

_____

_____

THE BEST PART WAS...

_____

_____

_____

_____

BUDGET

$ _____

ANTICIPATED DATE

/ /   TO   / /

ACTION LIST

⊘ _____
⊘ _____
⊘ _____
⊘ _____
⊘ _____
⊘ _____
⊘ _____
⊘ _____
⊘ _____

SUCCESS!

PLACE A CHECK HERE TO
TAKE IT OFF YOUR BUCKET LIST

RATE THIS ACTIVITY

☆☆☆☆☆

THIS WOULD BE PERFECT FOR US BECAUSE...

_____
_____
_____
_____

MAKE IT HAPPEN: HOW? WHEN?

_____
_____
_____
_____
_____

REVIEW
DATE COMPLETED: / /

WHAT HAPPENED? (PEOPLE MET, HIGH POINTS, CHALLENGES, EXPECTATIONS VS REALITY)

_____
_____
_____
_____

THE BEST PART WAS...

_____
_____
_____
_____

BUDGET

$

ANTICIPATED DATE

/ /   TO   / /

ACTION LIST

⊘ _____
⊘ _____
⊘ _____
⊘ _____
⊘ _____
⊘ _____
⊘ _____
⊘ _____
⊘ _____

SUCCESS!

PLACE A CHECK HERE TO
TAKE IT OFF YOUR BUCKET LIST

RATE THIS ACTIVITY

☆☆☆☆☆

ITEM #23: _____

THIS WOULD BE PERFECT FOR US BECAUSE...

_____
_____
_____

MAKE IT HAPPEN: HOW? WHEN?

_____
_____
_____
_____

REVIEW

DATE COMPLETED: / /

WHAT HAPPENED? (PEOPLE MET, HIGH POINTS, CHALLENGES, EXPECTATIONS VS REALITY)

_____
_____
_____
_____

THE BEST PART WAS...

_____
_____
_____
_____

BUDGET

$ _____

ANTICIPATED DATE

/ /   TO   / /

ACTION LIST

⊘ _____
⊘ _____
⊘ _____
⊘ _____
⊘ _____
⊘ _____
⊘ _____
⊘ _____
⊘ _____

SUCCESS!

PLACE A CHECK HERE TO
TAKE IT OFF YOUR BUCKET LIST

RATE THIS ACTIVITY

☆☆☆☆☆

THIS WOULD BE PERFECT FOR US BECAUSE...

_____
_____
_____
_____

MAKE IT HAPPEN: HOW? WHEN?

_____
_____
_____
_____

REVIEW

DATE COMPLETED: /   /

_____

WHAT HAPPENED? (PEOPLE MET, HIGH POINTS, CHALLENGES, EXPECTATIONS VS REALITY)

_____
_____
_____
_____
_____

THE BEST PART WAS...

_____
_____
_____
_____
_____

BUDGET

$

ANTICIPATED DATE

/ /   TO   / /

ACTION LIST

⊘ _____
⊘ _____
⊘ _____
⊘ _____
⊘ _____
⊘ _____
⊘ _____
⊘ _____
⊘ _____
⊘ _____

SUCCESS!

PLACE A CHECK HERE TO
TAKE IT OFF YOUR BUCKET LIST

RATE THIS ACTIVITY

☆☆☆☆☆

THIS WOULD BE PERFECT FOR US BECAUSE...

_____
_____
_____

MAKE IT HAPPEN: HOW? WHEN?

_____
_____
_____
_____

REVIEW

DATE COMPLETED: / /

WHAT HAPPENED? (PEOPLE MET, HIGH POINTS, CHALLENGES, EXPECTATIONS VS REALITY)

_____
_____
_____

THE BEST PART WAS...

_____
_____
_____
_____

BUDGET

$ _____

ANTICIPATED DATE

/ /   TO   / /

ACTION LIST

⊘ _____
⊘ _____
⊘ _____
⊘ _____
⊘ _____
⊘ _____
⊘ _____
⊘ _____
⊘ _____

(SUCCESS!)

PLACE A CHECK HERE TO
TAKE IT OFF YOUR BUCKET LIST

RATE THIS ACTIVITY

☆☆☆☆☆

THIS WOULD BE PERFECT FOR US BECAUSE...

_____
_____
_____
_____

MAKE IT HAPPEN: HOW? WHEN?

_____
_____
_____
_____
_____

REVIEW

DATE COMPLETED: / /

_____

WHAT HAPPENED? (PEOPLE MET, HIGH POINTS, CHALLENGES, EXPECTATIONS VS REALITY)

_____
_____
_____
_____

THE BEST PART WAS...

_____
_____
_____
_____
_____

BUDGET

$

ANTICIPATED DATE

/ /   TO   / /

ACTION LIST

⊘ _____
⊘ _____
⊘ _____
⊘ _____
⊘ _____
⊘ _____
⊘ _____
⊘ _____
⊘ _____

SUCCESS!

PLACE A CHECK HERE TO
TAKE IT OFF YOUR BUCKET LIST

RATE THIS ACTIVITY

☆☆☆☆☆

I'VE LEARNED THAT PEOPLE WILL FORGET WHAT YOU SAID, PEOPLE WILL FORGET WHAT YOU DID,
BUT PEOPLE WILL NEVER FORGET HOW YOU MADE THEM FEEL. – MAYA ANGELOU

ITEM #27: _____

THIS WOULD BE PERFECT FOR US BECAUSE...

_____

_____

_____

MAKE IT HAPPEN: HOW? WHEN?

_____

_____

_____

_____

REVIEW

DATE COMPLETED: / /

WHAT HAPPENED? (PEOPLE MET, HIGH POINTS, CHALLENGES, EXPECTATIONS VS REALITY)

_____

_____

_____

_____

THE BEST PART WAS...

_____

_____

_____

_____

BUDGET

$

ANTICIPATED DATE

/ / TO / /

ACTION LIST

⊘ _____
⊘ _____
⊘ _____
⊘ _____
⊘ _____
⊘ _____
⊘ _____
⊘ _____
⊘ _____

SUCCESS!

PLACE A CHECK HERE TO
TAKE IT OFF YOUR BUCKET LIST

RATE THIS ACTIVITY

☆☆☆☆☆

THIS WOULD BE PERFECT FOR US BECAUSE...

_____
_____
_____

MAKE IT HAPPEN: HOW? WHEN?

_____
_____
_____
_____

REVIEW

DATE COMPLETED: / /

WHAT HAPPENED? (PEOPLE MET, HIGH POINTS, CHALLENGES, EXPECTATIONS VS REALITY)

_____
_____
_____
_____

THE BEST PART WAS...

_____
_____
_____
_____

BUDGET

$

ANTICIPATED DATE

/ /   TO   / /

ACTION LIST

⊘ _____
⊘ _____
⊘ _____
⊘ _____
⊘ _____
⊘ _____
⊘ _____
⊘ _____
⊘ _____

SUCCESS!

PLACE A CHECK HERE TO
TAKE IT OFF YOUR BUCKET LIST

RATE THIS ACTIVITY

☆☆☆☆☆

THIS WOULD BE PERFECT FOR US BECAUSE...

MAKE IT HAPPEN: HOW? WHEN?

REVIEW

DATE COMPLETED: / /

WHAT HAPPENED? (PEOPLE MET, HIGH POINTS, CHALLENGES, EXPECTATIONS VS REALITY)

THE BEST PART WAS...

BUDGET

$

ANTICIPATED DATE

/ /   TO   / /

ACTION LIST

⊘ _____
⊘ _____
⊘ _____
⊘ _____
⊘ _____
⊘ _____
⊘ _____
⊘ _____
⊘ _____

SUCCESS!

PLACE A CHECK HERE TO
TAKE IT OFF YOUR BUCKET LIST

RATE THIS ACTIVITY

☆☆☆☆☆

THIS WOULD BE PERFECT FOR US BECAUSE...

_____
_____
_____
_____

MAKE IT HAPPEN: HOW? WHEN?

_____
_____
_____
_____
_____

REVIEW

DATE COMPLETED: / /

WHAT HAPPENED? (PEOPLE MET, HIGH POINTS, CHALLENGES, EXPECTATIONS VS REALITY)

_____
_____
_____
_____
_____

THE BEST PART WAS...

_____
_____
_____
_____
_____

BUDGET

$

ANTICIPATED DATE

/ /   TO   / /

ACTION LIST

⊘ _____
⊘ _____
⊘ _____
⊘ _____
⊘ _____
⊘ _____
⊘ _____
⊘ _____
⊘ _____

SUCCESS!

PLACE A CHECK HERE TO
TAKE IT OFF YOUR BUCKET LIST

RATE THIS ACTIVITY

☆☆☆☆☆

WHATEVER YOU CAN DO, OR DREAM YOU CAN, BEGIN IT... BOLDNESS HAS GENIUS,
POWER AND MAGIC IN IT. — JOHANN WOLFGANG VON GOETHE

PRIORITY ☆☆☆☆☆ ITEM #31: _____

THIS WOULD BE PERFECT FOR US BECAUSE...	**BUDGET**
	$
	ANTICIPATED DATE
	/ / TO / /
MAKE IT HAPPEN: HOW? WHEN?	**ACTION LIST**
	⊘ _____
	⊘ _____
	⊘ _____
	⊘ _____
REVIEW	⊘ _____
DATE COMPLETED: / /	⊘ _____
	⊘ _____
WHAT HAPPENED? (PEOPLE MET, HIGH POINTS, CHALLENGES, EXPECTATIONS VS REALITY)	⊘ _____
	⊘ _____
	SUCCESS!
THE BEST PART WAS...	
	PLACE A CHECK HERE TO TAKE IT OFF YOUR BUCKET LIST
	RATE THIS ACTIVITY
	☆☆☆☆☆

THIS WOULD BE PERFECT FOR US BECAUSE...

_____

_____

_____

MAKE IT HAPPEN: HOW? WHEN?

_____

_____

_____

_____

REVIEW

DATE COMPLETED: / /

WHAT HAPPENED? (PEOPLE MET, HIGH POINTS, CHALLENGES, EXPECTATIONS VS REALITY)

_____

_____

_____

_____

THE BEST PART WAS...

_____

_____

_____

_____

_____

BUDGET

$

ANTICIPATED DATE

/ /   TO   / /

ACTION LIST

⊘ _____

⊘ _____

⊘ _____

⊘ _____

⊘ _____

⊘ _____

⊘ _____

⊘ _____

⊘ _____

SUCCESS!

PLACE A CHECK HERE TO
TAKE IT OFF YOUR BUCKET LIST

RATE THIS ACTIVITY

☆☆☆☆☆

PRIORITY ☆☆☆☆☆   ITEM #33: _____

THIS WOULD BE PERFECT FOR US BECAUSE...	BUDGET

THIS WOULD BE PERFECT FOR US BECAUSE...
_____
_____
_____

BUDGET

$

ANTICIPATED DATE

/ /   TO   / /

MAKE IT HAPPEN: HOW? WHEN?
_____
_____
_____
_____

ACTION LIST

⊘ _____
⊘ _____
⊘ _____
⊘ _____
⊘ _____
⊘ _____
⊘ _____
⊘ _____
⊘ _____

REVIEW
DATE COMPLETED: / /

WHAT HAPPENED? (PEOPLE MET, HIGH POINTS, CHALLENGES, EXPECTATIONS VS REALITY)
_____
_____
_____
_____

(SUCCESS!)

THE BEST PART WAS...
_____
_____
_____
_____

PLACE A CHECK HERE TO
TAKE IT OFF YOUR BUCKET LIST

RATE THIS ACTIVITY

☆☆☆☆☆

THIS WOULD BE PERFECT FOR US BECAUSE...

_____

_____

_____

MAKE IT HAPPEN: HOW? WHEN?

_____

_____

_____

_____

REVIEW

DATE COMPLETED: / /

WHAT HAPPENED? (PEOPLE MET, HIGH POINTS, CHALLENGES, EXPECTATIONS VS REALITY)

_____

_____

_____

_____

THE BEST PART WAS...

_____

_____

_____

_____

BUDGET

$

ANTICIPATED DATE

/ /   TO   / /

ACTION LIST

⊘ _____
⊘ _____
⊘ _____
⊘ _____
⊘ _____
⊘ _____
⊘ _____
⊘ _____
⊘ _____

SUCCESS!

PLACE A CHECK HERE TO
TAKE IT OFF YOUR BUCKET LIST

RATE THIS ACTIVITY

☆☆☆☆☆

IF YOU HEAR A VOICE WITHIN YOU SAY "YOU CANNOT PAINT," THEN BY ALL MEANS
PAINT AND THAT VOICE WILL BE SILENCED. — VINCENT VAN GOGH

THIS WOULD BE PERFECT FOR US BECAUSE...

_____
_____
_____
_____

MAKE IT HAPPEN: HOW? WHEN?

_____
_____
_____
_____
_____

REVIEW

DATE COMPLETED: / /

WHAT HAPPENED? (PEOPLE MET, HIGH POINTS, CHALLENGES, EXPECTATIONS VS REALITY)

_____
_____
_____
_____

THE BEST PART WAS...

_____
_____
_____
_____
_____

BUDGET

$ _____

ANTICIPATED DATE

/ /   TO   / /

ACTION LIST

⊘ _____
⊘ _____
⊘ _____
⊘ _____
⊘ _____
⊘ _____
⊘ _____
⊘ _____
⊘ _____

(SUCCESS!)

PLACE A CHECK HERE TO
TAKE IT OFF YOUR BUCKET LIST

RATE THIS ACTIVITY

☆☆☆☆☆

THIS WOULD BE PERFECT FOR US BECAUSE...

MAKE IT HAPPEN: HOW? WHEN?

REVIEW
DATE COMPLETED: /   /

WHAT HAPPENED? (PEOPLE MET, HIGH POINTS, CHALLENGES, EXPECTATIONS VS REALITY)

THE BEST PART WAS...

BUDGET

$

ANTICIPATED DATE

/   /   TO   /   /

ACTION LIST

⊘ _____
⊘ _____
⊘ _____
⊘ _____
⊘ _____
⊘ _____
⊘ _____
⊘ _____
⊘ _____

SUCCESS!

PLACE A CHECK HERE TO
TAKE IT OFF YOUR BUCKET LIST

RATE THIS ACTIVITY

☆☆☆☆☆

ASK AND IT WILL BE GIVEN TO YOU; SEARCH, AND YOU WILL FIND; KNOCK AND THE DOOR WILL BE OPENED FOR YOU. – JESUS

THIS WOULD BE PERFECT FOR US BECAUSE...

BUDGET

$

ANTICIPATED DATE

/ /   TO   / /

MAKE IT HAPPEN: HOW? WHEN?

ACTION LIST

⊘
⊘
⊘
⊘
⊘
⊘
⊘
⊘
⊘

REVIEW

DATE COMPLETED: / /

WHAT HAPPENED? (PEOPLE MET, HIGH POINTS, CHALLENGES, EXPECTATIONS VS REALITY)

SUCCESS!

PLACE A CHECK HERE TO
TAKE IT OFF YOUR BUCKET LIST

RATE THIS ACTIVITY

☆☆☆☆☆

THE BEST PART WAS...

ITEM #38: _____

THIS WOULD BE PERFECT FOR US BECAUSE...

_____
_____
_____
_____

MAKE IT HAPPEN: HOW? WHEN?

_____
_____
_____
_____
_____

REVIEW
DATE COMPLETED: / /

WHAT HAPPENED? (PEOPLE MET, HIGH POINTS, CHALLENGES, EXPECTATIONS VS REALITY)

_____
_____
_____
_____
_____

THE BEST PART WAS...

_____
_____
_____
_____
_____

BUDGET

$

ANTICIPATED DATE

/ / TO / /

ACTION LIST

⊘ _____
⊘ _____
⊘ _____
⊘ _____
⊘ _____
⊘ _____
⊘ _____
⊘ _____
⊘ _____

SUCCESS!

PLACE A CHECK HERE TO
TAKE IT OFF YOUR BUCKET LIST

RATE THIS ACTIVITY

☆☆☆☆☆

GO CONFIDENTLY IN THE DIRECTION OF YOUR DREAMS... LIVE THE LIFE YOU HAVE IMAGINED. — HENRY DAVID THOREAU

THIS WOULD BE PERFECT FOR US BECAUSE...

BUDGET

$

ANTICIPATED DATE

/ /   TO   / /

MAKE IT HAPPEN: HOW? WHEN?

ACTION LIST

⊘ _____
⊘ _____
⊘ _____
⊘ _____
⊘ _____
⊘ _____
⊘ _____
⊘ _____
⊘ _____

REVIEW

DATE COMPLETED: / /

WHAT HAPPENED? (PEOPLE MET, HIGH POINTS, CHALLENGES, EXPECTATIONS VS REALITY)

SUCCESS!

PLACE A CHECK HERE TO
TAKE IT OFF YOUR BUCKET LIST

THE BEST PART WAS...

RATE THIS ACTIVITY

☆☆☆☆☆

WHEN I STAND BEFORE GOD AT THE END OF MY LIFE, I WOULD HOPE THAT I WOULD NOT HAVE A SINGLE BIT
OF TALENT LEFT AND COULD SAY, I USED EVERYTHING YOU GAVE ME. — ERMA BOMBECK

THIS WOULD BE PERFECT FOR US BECAUSE...

BUDGET

$

ANTICIPATED DATE

/ /   TO   / /

MAKE IT HAPPEN: HOW? WHEN?

ACTION LIST

⊘ _____
⊘ _____
⊘ _____
⊘ _____
⊘ _____
⊘ _____
⊘ _____
⊘ _____
⊘ _____

REVIEW

DATE COMPLETED: / /

WHAT HAPPENED? (PEOPLE MET, HIGH POINTS, CHALLENGES, EXPECTATIONS VS REALITY)

SUCCESS!

PLACE A CHECK HERE TO
TAKE IT OFF YOUR BUCKET LIST

THE BEST PART WAS...

RATE THIS ACTIVITY

☆☆☆☆☆

ITEM #41: _____

THIS WOULD BE PERFECT FOR US BECAUSE...

_____
_____
_____

MAKE IT HAPPEN: HOW? WHEN?

_____
_____
_____
_____

REVIEW

DATE COMPLETED: / /

WHAT HAPPENED? (PEOPLE MET, HIGH POINTS, CHALLENGES, EXPECTATIONS VS REALITY)

_____
_____
_____
_____

THE BEST PART WAS...

_____
_____
_____
_____

BUDGET

$

ANTICIPATED DATE

/ /   TO   / /

ACTION LIST

⊘ _____
⊘ _____
⊘ _____
⊘ _____
⊘ _____
⊘ _____
⊘ _____
⊘ _____
⊘ _____

SUCCESS!

PLACE A CHECK HERE TO
TAKE IT OFF YOUR BUCKET LIST

RATE THIS ACTIVITY

☆☆☆☆☆

CERTAIN THINGS CATCH YOUR EYE, BUT PURSUE ONLY THOSE THAT CAPTURE THE HEART. — ANCIENT INDIAN PROVERB

THIS WOULD BE PERFECT FOR US BECAUSE...

MAKE IT HAPPEN: HOW? WHEN?

REVIEW
DATE COMPLETED: / /

WHAT HAPPENED? (PEOPLE MET, HIGH POINTS, CHALLENGES, EXPECTATIONS VS REALITY)

THE BEST PART WAS...

BUDGET

$

ANTICIPATED DATE

/ /   TO   / /

ACTION LIST

⊘ _____
⊘ _____
⊘ _____
⊘ _____
⊘ _____
⊘ _____
⊘ _____
⊘ _____
⊘ _____

SUCCESS!

PLACE A CHECK HERE TO
TAKE IT OFF YOUR BUCKET LIST

RATE THIS ACTIVITY

☆☆☆☆☆

PRIORITY ☆☆☆☆☆   ITEM #43: _____

THIS WOULD BE PERFECT FOR US BECAUSE...

_____
_____
_____

MAKE IT HAPPEN: HOW? WHEN?

_____
_____
_____
_____

REVIEW

DATE COMPLETED: / /

WHAT HAPPENED? (PEOPLE MET, HIGH POINTS, CHALLENGES, EXPECTATIONS VS REALITY)

_____
_____
_____
_____

THE BEST PART WAS...

_____
_____
_____
_____

BUDGET

$

ANTICIPATED DATE

/ /   TO   / /

ACTION LIST

⊘ _____
⊘ _____
⊘ _____
⊘ _____
⊘ _____
⊘ _____
⊘ _____
⊘ _____
⊘ _____

SUCCESS!

PLACE A CHECK HERE TO
TAKE IT OFF YOUR BUCKET LIST

RATE THIS ACTIVITY

☆☆☆☆☆

THIS WOULD BE PERFECT FOR US BECAUSE...

_____
_____
_____
_____

MAKE IT HAPPEN: HOW? WHEN?

_____
_____
_____
_____
_____

REVIEW

DATE COMPLETED: / /

_____

WHAT HAPPENED? (PEOPLE MET, HIGH POINTS, CHALLENGES, EXPECTATIONS VS REALITY)

_____
_____
_____
_____
_____

THE BEST PART WAS...

_____
_____
_____
_____
_____

BUDGET

$

ANTICIPATED DATE

/ /   TO   / /

ACTION LIST

⊘ _____
⊘ _____
⊘ _____
⊘ _____
⊘ _____
⊘ _____
⊘ _____
⊘ _____
⊘ _____

SUCCESS!

PLACE A CHECK HERE TO
TAKE IT OFF YOUR BUCKET LIST

RATE THIS ACTIVITY

☆☆☆☆☆

THIS WOULD BE PERFECT FOR US BECAUSE...

_____
_____
_____
_____

MAKE IT HAPPEN: HOW? WHEN?

_____
_____
_____
_____
_____

REVIEW

DATE COMPLETED: / /

WHAT HAPPENED? (PEOPLE MET, HIGH POINTS, CHALLENGES, EXPECTATIONS VS REALITY)

_____
_____
_____
_____
_____

THE BEST PART WAS...

_____
_____
_____
_____
_____

BUDGET

$

ANTICIPATED DATE

/ /   TO   / /

ACTION LIST

⊘ _____
⊘ _____
⊘ _____
⊘ _____
⊘ _____
⊘ _____
⊘ _____
⊘ _____
⊘ _____

SUCCESS!

PLACE A CHECK HERE TO
TAKE IT OFF YOUR BUCKET LIST

RATE THIS ACTIVITY

☆☆☆☆☆

THIS WOULD BE PERFECT FOR US BECAUSE...

_____
_____
_____
_____

MAKE IT HAPPEN: HOW? WHEN?

_____
_____
_____
_____
_____

REVIEW
DATE COMPLETED: / /

WHAT HAPPENED? (PEOPLE MET, HIGH POINTS, CHALLENGES, EXPECTATIONS VS REALITY)

_____
_____
_____
_____
_____

THE BEST PART WAS...

_____
_____
_____
_____
_____

BUDGET

$

ANTICIPATED DATE

/ /   TO   / /

ACTION LIST

⊘ _____
⊘ _____
⊘ _____
⊘ _____
⊘ _____
⊘ _____
⊘ _____
⊘ _____
⊘ _____

SUCCESS!

PLACE A CHECK HERE TO
TAKE IT OFF YOUR BUCKET LIST

RATE THIS ACTIVITY

☆☆☆☆☆

ITEM #47: _____

THIS WOULD BE PERFECT FOR US BECAUSE...

_____

_____

_____

_____

MAKE IT HAPPEN: HOW? WHEN?

_____

_____

_____

_____

REVIEW

DATE COMPLETED: / /

WHAT HAPPENED? (PEOPLE MET, HIGH POINTS, CHALLENGES, EXPECTATIONS VS REALITY)

_____

_____

_____

_____

THE BEST PART WAS...

_____

_____

_____

_____

BUDGET

$

ANTICIPATED DATE

/ /   TO   / /

ACTION LIST

⊘ _____
⊘ _____
⊘ _____
⊘ _____
⊘ _____
⊘ _____
⊘ _____
⊘ _____
⊘ _____

SUCCESS!

PLACE A CHECK HERE TO
TAKE IT OFF YOUR BUCKET LIST

RATE THIS ACTIVITY

☆☆☆☆☆

FALL SEVEN TIMES AND STAND UP EIGHT. – JAPANESE PROVERB

THIS WOULD BE PERFECT FOR US BECAUSE...

_____

_____

_____

MAKE IT HAPPEN: HOW? WHEN?

_____

_____

_____

_____

REVIEW

DATE COMPLETED: / /

WHAT HAPPENED? (PEOPLE MET, HIGH POINTS, CHALLENGES, EXPECTATIONS VS REALITY)

_____

_____

_____

_____

THE BEST PART WAS...

_____

_____

_____

_____

BUDGET

$

ANTICIPATED DATE

/ /   TO   / /

ACTION LIST

⊘ _____
⊘ _____
⊘ _____
⊘ _____
⊘ _____
⊘ _____
⊘ _____
⊘ _____
⊘ _____

SUCCESS!

PLACE A CHECK HERE TO
TAKE IT OFF YOUR BUCKET LIST

RATE THIS ACTIVITY

☆☆☆☆☆

ITEM #49: _____

THIS WOULD BE PERFECT FOR US BECAUSE...

_____
_____
_____
_____

MAKE IT HAPPEN: HOW? WHEN?

_____
_____
_____
_____
_____
_____

REVIEW

DATE COMPLETED: / /

WHAT HAPPENED? (PEOPLE MET, HIGH POINTS, CHALLENGES, EXPECTATIONS VS REALITY)

_____
_____
_____
_____
_____

THE BEST PART WAS...

_____
_____
_____
_____
_____

BUDGET

$

ANTICIPATED DATE

/ /   TO   / /

ACTION LIST

⊘ _____
⊘ _____
⊘ _____
⊘ _____
⊘ _____
⊘ _____
⊘ _____
⊘ _____
⊘ _____

SUCCESS!

PLACE A CHECK HERE TO
TAKE IT OFF YOUR BUCKET LIST

RATE THIS ACTIVITY

☆☆☆☆☆

ITEM #50: _____

THIS WOULD BE PERFECT FOR US BECAUSE…

_____
_____
_____
_____

MAKE IT HAPPEN: HOW? WHEN?

_____
_____
_____
_____
_____

REVIEW
DATE COMPLETED: / /

WHAT HAPPENED? (PEOPLE MET, HIGH POINTS, CHALLENGES, EXPECTATIONS VS REALITY)

_____
_____
_____
_____
_____

THE BEST PART WAS…

_____
_____
_____
_____
_____

BUDGET
$ _____

ANTICIPATED DATE
/ /   TO   / /

ACTION LIST
⊘ _____
⊘ _____
⊘ _____
⊘ _____
⊘ _____
⊘ _____
⊘ _____
⊘ _____
⊘ _____

SUCCESS!

PLACE A CHECK HERE TO
TAKE IT OFF YOUR BUCKET LIST

RATE THIS ACTIVITY

☆☆☆☆☆

HOW WONDERFUL IT IS THAT NOBODY NEED WAIT A SINGLE MOMENT
BEFORE STARTING TO IMPROVE THE WORLD. — ANNE FRANK

ITEM #51: _____

THIS WOULD BE PERFECT FOR US BECAUSE...

_____
_____
_____

MAKE IT HAPPEN: HOW? WHEN?

_____
_____
_____
_____
_____

REVIEW

DATE COMPLETED: / /

_____

WHAT HAPPENED? (PEOPLE MET, HIGH POINTS, CHALLENGES, EXPECTATIONS VS REALITY)

_____
_____
_____
_____

THE BEST PART WAS...

_____
_____
_____
_____
_____

BUDGET

$

ANTICIPATED DATE

/ /   TO   / /

ACTION LIST

⊘ _____
⊘ _____
⊘ _____
⊘ _____
⊘ _____
⊘ _____
⊘ _____
⊘ _____
⊘ _____

SUCCESS!

PLACE A CHECK HERE TO
TAKE IT OFF YOUR BUCKET LIST

RATE THIS ACTIVITY

☆☆☆☆☆

WHEN I LET GO OF WHAT I AM, I BECOME WHAT I MIGHT BE. — LAO TZU

ITEM #52: _____

THIS WOULD BE PERFECT FOR US BECAUSE...

_____
_____
_____
_____

MAKE IT HAPPEN: HOW? WHEN?

_____
_____
_____
_____
_____

REVIEW

DATE COMPLETED: / /

WHAT HAPPENED? (PEOPLE MET, HIGH POINTS, CHALLENGES, EXPECTATIONS VS REALITY)

_____
_____
_____
_____
_____

THE BEST PART WAS...

_____
_____
_____
_____
_____

BUDGET

$

ANTICIPATED DATE

/ /   TO   / /

ACTION LIST

⊘ _____
⊘ _____
⊘ _____
⊘ _____
⊘ _____
⊘ _____
⊘ _____
⊘ _____
⊘ _____

SUCCESS!

PLACE A CHECK HERE TO
TAKE IT OFF YOUR BUCKET LIST

RATE THIS ACTIVITY

☆☆☆☆☆

ITEM #53: _____

THIS WOULD BE PERFECT FOR US BECAUSE...
_____
_____
_____
_____

MAKE IT HAPPEN: HOW? WHEN?
_____
_____
_____
_____
_____

REVIEW

DATE COMPLETED: / /

WHAT HAPPENED? (PEOPLE MET, HIGH POINTS, CHALLENGES, EXPECTATIONS VS REALITY)
_____
_____
_____
_____

THE BEST PART WAS...
_____
_____
_____
_____
_____
_____

BUDGET

$ _____

ANTICIPATED DATE

/ / TO / /

ACTION LIST

⊘ _____
⊘ _____
⊘ _____
⊘ _____
⊘ _____
⊘ _____
⊘ _____
⊘ _____
⊘ _____

SUCCESS!

PLACE A CHECK HERE TO
TAKE IT OFF YOUR BUCKET LIST

RATE THIS ACTIVITY

☆☆☆☆☆

THIS WOULD BE PERFECT FOR US BECAUSE...

MAKE IT HAPPEN: HOW? WHEN?

REVIEW
DATE COMPLETED: / /

WHAT HAPPENED? (PEOPLE MET, HIGH POINTS, CHALLENGES, EXPECTATIONS VS REALITY)

THE BEST PART WAS...

BUDGET

$

ANTICIPATED DATE

/ /   TO   / /

ACTION LIST

- ⊘
- ⊘
- ⊘
- ⊘
- ⊘
- ⊘
- ⊘
- ⊘
- ⊘

SUCCESS!

PLACE A CHECK HERE TO
TAKE IT OFF YOUR BUCKET LIST

RATE THIS ACTIVITY

☆☆☆☆☆

ITEM #55: _____

THIS WOULD BE PERFECT FOR US BECAUSE...

_____
_____
_____

MAKE IT HAPPEN: HOW? WHEN?

_____
_____
_____
_____
_____
_____

REVIEW

DATE COMPLETED: / /

WHAT HAPPENED? (PEOPLE MET, HIGH POINTS, CHALLENGES, EXPECTATIONS VS REALITY)

_____
_____
_____
_____
_____

THE BEST PART WAS...

_____
_____
_____
_____

BUDGET

$

ANTICIPATED DATE

/ / TO / /

ACTION LIST

⊘ _____
⊘ _____
⊘ _____
⊘ _____
⊘ _____
⊘ _____
⊘ _____
⊘ _____
⊘ _____

SUCCESS!

PLACE A CHECK HERE TO
TAKE IT OFF YOUR BUCKET LIST

RATE THIS ACTIVITY

☆☆☆☆☆

FIRST, HAVE A DEFINITE, CLEAR PRACTICAL IDEAL; A GOAL, AN OBJECTIVE / SECOND, HAVE THE NECESSARY MEANS TO ACHIEVE
YOUR ENDS; WISDOM, MONEY, MATERIALS, AND METHODS / THIRD: ADJUST ALL YOUR MEANS TO THAT END. – ARISTOTLE

THIS WOULD BE PERFECT FOR US BECAUSE...

MAKE IT HAPPEN: HOW? WHEN?

REVIEW
DATE COMPLETED: / /

WHAT HAPPENED? (PEOPLE MET, HIGH POINTS, CHALLENGES, EXPECTATIONS VS REALITY)

THE BEST PART WAS...

BUDGET

$

ANTICIPATED DATE

/ /   TO   / /

ACTION LIST

⊘ _____
⊘ _____
⊘ _____
⊘ _____
⊘ _____
⊘ _____
⊘ _____
⊘ _____
⊘ _____

SUCCESS!

PLACE A CHECK HERE TO
TAKE IT OFF YOUR BUCKET LIST

RATE THIS ACTIVITY

☆☆☆☆☆

THIS WOULD BE PERFECT FOR US BECAUSE...

_____
_____
_____
_____

MAKE IT HAPPEN: HOW? WHEN?

_____
_____
_____
_____
_____

REVIEW

DATE COMPLETED: / /

WHAT HAPPENED? (PEOPLE MET, HIGH POINTS, CHALLENGES, EXPECTATIONS VS REALITY)

_____
_____
_____
_____
_____

THE BEST PART WAS...

_____
_____
_____
_____

BUDGET

$

ANTICIPATED DATE

/ /   TO   / /

ACTION LIST

⊘ _____
⊘ _____
⊘ _____
⊘ _____
⊘ _____
⊘ _____
⊘ _____
⊘ _____
⊘ _____

SUCCESS!

PLACE A CHECK HERE TO
TAKE IT OFF YOUR BUCKET LIST

RATE THIS ACTIVITY

☆☆☆☆☆

THIS WOULD BE PERFECT FOR US BECAUSE...

BUDGET

$

ANTICIPATED DATE

/ /   TO   / /

MAKE IT HAPPEN: HOW? WHEN?

ACTION LIST

⊘ _____
⊘ _____
⊘ _____
⊘ _____
⊘ _____
⊘ _____
⊘ _____
⊘ _____
⊘ _____

REVIEW

DATE COMPLETED: / /

WHAT HAPPENED? (PEOPLE MET, HIGH POINTS, CHALLENGES, EXPECTATIONS VS REALITY)

SUCCESS!

PLACE A CHECK HERE TO
TAKE IT OFF YOUR BUCKET LIST

THE BEST PART WAS...

RATE THIS ACTIVITY

☆☆☆☆☆

THIS WOULD BE PERFECT FOR US BECAUSE...

BUDGET

$

ANTICIPATED DATE

/ /   TO   / /

MAKE IT HAPPEN: HOW? WHEN?

ACTION LIST

⊘ _____
⊘ _____
⊘ _____
⊘ _____
⊘ _____
⊘ _____
⊘ _____
⊘ _____
⊘ _____

REVIEW

DATE COMPLETED: / /

WHAT HAPPENED? (PEOPLE MET, HIGH POINTS, CHALLENGES, EXPECTATIONS VS REALITY)

SUCCESS!

PLACE A CHECK HERE TO
TAKE IT OFF YOUR BUCKET LIST

RATE THIS ACTIVITY

☆☆☆☆☆

THE BEST PART WAS...

THIS WOULD BE PERFECT FOR US BECAUSE...

_____
_____
_____
_____

MAKE IT HAPPEN: HOW? WHEN?

_____
_____
_____
_____
_____

REVIEW
DATE COMPLETED: / /

WHAT HAPPENED? (PEOPLE MET, HIGH POINTS, CHALLENGES, EXPECTATIONS VS REALITY)

_____
_____
_____
_____
_____

THE BEST PART WAS...

_____
_____
_____
_____
_____

BUDGET

$

ANTICIPATED DATE

/ /   TO   / /

ACTION LIST

⊘ _____
⊘ _____
⊘ _____
⊘ _____
⊘ _____
⊘ _____
⊘ _____
⊘ _____
⊘ _____

SUCCESS!

PLACE A CHECK HERE TO
TAKE IT OFF YOUR BUCKET LIST

RATE THIS ACTIVITY

☆☆☆☆☆

CHALLENGES ARE WHAT MAKE LIFE INTERESTING AND OVERCOMING THEM
IS WHAT MAKES LIFE MEANINGFUL. — JOSHUA J. MARINE

THIS WOULD BE PERFECT FOR US BECAUSE...

_____

_____

_____

MAKE IT HAPPEN: HOW? WHEN?

_____

_____

_____

_____

REVIEW

DATE COMPLETED: / /

WHAT HAPPENED? (PEOPLE MET, HIGH POINTS, CHALLENGES, EXPECTATIONS VS REALITY)

_____

_____

_____

THE BEST PART WAS...

_____

_____

_____

_____

BUDGET

$

ANTICIPATED DATE

/ /   TO   / /

ACTION LIST

⊘ _____
⊘ _____
⊘ _____
⊘ _____
⊘ _____
⊘ _____
⊘ _____
⊘ _____
⊘ _____

SUCCESS!

PLACE A CHECK HERE TO
TAKE IT OFF YOUR BUCKET LIST

RATE THIS ACTIVITY

☆☆☆☆☆

THIS WOULD BE PERFECT FOR US BECAUSE...

MAKE IT HAPPEN: HOW? WHEN?

REVIEW
DATE COMPLETED: / /

WHAT HAPPENED? (PEOPLE MET, HIGH POINTS, CHALLENGES, EXPECTATIONS VS REALITY)

THE BEST PART WAS...

BUDGET

$

ANTICIPATED DATE

/ /   TO   / /

ACTION LIST

- ⊘ _____
- ⊘ _____
- ⊘ _____
- ⊘ _____
- ⊘ _____
- ⊘ _____
- ⊘ _____
- ⊘ _____
- ⊘ _____

SUCCESS!

PLACE A CHECK HERE TO
TAKE IT OFF YOUR BUCKET LIST

RATE THIS ACTIVITY

☆☆☆☆☆

I HAVE BEEN IMPRESSED WITH THE URGENCY OF DOING; KNOWING IS NOT ENOUGH; WE MUST
APPLY! BEING WILLING IS NOT ENOUGH; WE MUST DO. – LEONARDO DA VINCI

THIS WOULD BE PERFECT FOR US BECAUSE...

_____

_____

_____

MAKE IT HAPPEN: HOW? WHEN?

_____

_____

_____

_____

_____

REVIEW

DATE COMPLETED: / /

_____

WHAT HAPPENED? (PEOPLE MET, HIGH POINTS, CHALLENGES, EXPECTATIONS VS REALITY)

_____

_____

_____

_____

_____

THE BEST PART WAS...

_____

_____

_____

_____

BUDGET

$

ANTICIPATED DATE

/ /   TO   / /

ACTION LIST

- ⊘ _____
- ⊘ _____
- ⊘ _____
- ⊘ _____
- ⊘ _____
- ⊘ _____
- ⊘ _____
- ⊘ _____
- ⊘ _____

SUCCESS!

PLACE A CHECK HERE TO
TAKE IT OFF YOUR BUCKET LIST

RATE THIS ACTIVITY

☆☆☆☆☆

THIS WOULD BE PERFECT FOR US BECAUSE...

MAKE IT HAPPEN: HOW? WHEN?

REVIEW
DATE COMPLETED: / /

WHAT HAPPENED? (PEOPLE MET, HIGH POINTS, CHALLENGES, EXPECTATIONS VS REALITY)

THE BEST PART WAS...

BUDGET

$

ANTICIPATED DATE

/ /   TO   / /

ACTION LIST

- ⊘ _____
- ⊘ _____
- ⊘ _____
- ⊘ _____
- ⊘ _____
- ⊘ _____
- ⊘ _____
- ⊘ _____
- ⊘ _____

SUCCESS!

PLACE A CHECK HERE TO
TAKE IT OFF YOUR BUCKET LIST

RATE THIS ACTIVITY

☆☆☆☆☆

YOU TAKE YOUR LIFE IN YOUR OWN HANDS, AND WHAT HAPPENS? A TERRIBLE THING, NO ONE TO BLAME. — ERICA JONG

THIS WOULD BE PERFECT FOR US BECAUSE...

_____
_____
_____
_____

MAKE IT HAPPEN: HOW? WHEN?

_____
_____
_____
_____
_____

REVIEW

DATE COMPLETED: /   /

WHAT HAPPENED? (PEOPLE MET, HIGH POINTS, CHALLENGES, EXPECTATIONS VS REALITY)

_____
_____
_____
_____

THE BEST PART WAS...

_____
_____
_____
_____
_____

BUDGET

$

ANTICIPATED DATE

/ /   TO   / /

ACTION LIST

⊘ _____
⊘ _____
⊘ _____
⊘ _____
⊘ _____
⊘ _____
⊘ _____
⊘ _____
⊘ _____

(SUCCESS!)

PLACE A CHECK HERE TO
TAKE IT OFF YOUR BUCKET LIST

RATE THIS ACTIVITY

☆☆☆☆☆

WHAT'S MONEY? A MAN IS A SUCCESS IF HE GETS UP IN THE MORNING AND GOES TO BED AT
NIGHT AND IN BETWEEN DOES WHAT HE WANTS TO DO. – BOB DYLAN

THIS WOULD BE PERFECT FOR US BECAUSE...

_____

_____

_____

MAKE IT HAPPEN: HOW? WHEN?

_____

_____

_____

_____

_____

REVIEW
DATE COMPLETED: / /

_____

WHAT HAPPENED? (PEOPLE MET, HIGH POINTS, CHALLENGES, EXPECTATIONS VS REALITY)

_____

_____

_____

_____

_____

THE BEST PART WAS...

_____

_____

_____

_____

_____

BUDGET

$

ANTICIPATED DATE

/ /   TO   / /

ACTION LIST

⊘ _____
⊘ _____
⊘ _____
⊘ _____
⊘ _____
⊘ _____
⊘ _____
⊘ _____
⊘ _____

SUCCESS!

PLACE A CHECK HERE TO
TAKE IT OFF YOUR BUCKET LIST

RATE THIS ACTIVITY

☆☆☆☆☆

ITEM #67: _____

THIS WOULD BE PERFECT FOR US BECAUSE...

_____
_____
_____

MAKE IT HAPPEN: HOW? WHEN?

_____
_____
_____
_____
_____

REVIEW

DATE COMPLETED: / /

WHAT HAPPENED? (PEOPLE MET, HIGH POINTS, CHALLENGES, EXPECTATIONS VS REALITY)

_____
_____
_____
_____
_____
_____

THE BEST PART WAS...

_____
_____
_____
_____

BUDGET

$

ANTICIPATED DATE

/ / TO / /

ACTION LIST

⊘ _____
⊘ _____
⊘ _____
⊘ _____
⊘ _____
⊘ _____
⊘ _____
⊘ _____
⊘ _____

SUCCESS!

PLACE A CHECK HERE TO
TAKE IT OFF YOUR BUCKET LIST

RATE THIS ACTIVITY

☆☆☆☆☆

ITEM #68: _____

THIS WOULD BE PERFECT FOR US BECAUSE...

_____

_____

_____

MAKE IT HAPPEN: HOW? WHEN?

_____

_____

_____

_____

_____

REVIEW
DATE COMPLETED: / /

WHAT HAPPENED? (PEOPLE MET, HIGH POINTS, CHALLENGES, EXPECTATIONS VS REALITY)

_____

_____

_____

_____

THE BEST PART WAS...

_____

_____

_____

_____

_____

BUDGET

$

ANTICIPATED DATE

/ /   TO   / /

ACTION LIST

⊘ _____
⊘ _____
⊘ _____
⊘ _____
⊘ _____
⊘ _____
⊘ _____
⊘ _____
⊘ _____

SUCCESS!

PLACE A CHECK HERE TO
TAKE IT OFF YOUR BUCKET LIST

RATE THIS ACTIVITY

☆☆☆☆☆

THIS WOULD BE PERFECT FOR US BECAUSE...

_____
_____
_____

MAKE IT HAPPEN: HOW? WHEN?

_____
_____
_____
_____
_____

REVIEW

DATE COMPLETED: /   /

WHAT HAPPENED? (PEOPLE MET, HIGH POINTS, CHALLENGES, EXPECTATIONS VS REALITY)

_____
_____
_____
_____
_____

THE BEST PART WAS...

_____
_____
_____
_____

BUDGET

$

ANTICIPATED DATE

/   /   TO   /   /

ACTION LIST

⊘ _____
⊘ _____
⊘ _____
⊘ _____
⊘ _____
⊘ _____
⊘ _____
⊘ _____
⊘ _____

(SUCCESS!)

PLACE A CHECK HERE TO
TAKE IT OFF YOUR BUCKET LIST

RATE THIS ACTIVITY

☆☆☆☆☆

THIS WOULD BE PERFECT FOR US BECAUSE...

BUDGET

$

ANTICIPATED DATE

/ /   TO   / /

MAKE IT HAPPEN: HOW? WHEN?

ACTION LIST

⊘ _____
⊘ _____
⊘ _____
⊘ _____
⊘ _____
⊘ _____
⊘ _____
⊘ _____
⊘ _____

REVIEW
DATE COMPLETED: / /

WHAT HAPPENED? (PEOPLE MET, HIGH POINTS, CHALLENGES, EXPECTATIONS VS REALITY)

SUCCESS!

PLACE A CHECK HERE TO
TAKE IT OFF YOUR BUCKET LIST

THE BEST PART WAS...

RATE THIS ACTIVITY

☆☆☆☆☆

THIS WOULD BE PERFECT FOR US BECAUSE...

MAKE IT HAPPEN: HOW? WHEN?

REVIEW

DATE COMPLETED: / /

WHAT HAPPENED? (PEOPLE MET, HIGH POINTS, CHALLENGES, EXPECTATIONS VS REALITY)

THE BEST PART WAS...

BUDGET

$

ANTICIPATED DATE

/ /   TO   / /

ACTION LIST

⊘ _____
⊘ _____
⊘ _____
⊘ _____
⊘ _____
⊘ _____
⊘ _____
⊘ _____
⊘ _____

SUCCESS!

PLACE A CHECK HERE TO
TAKE IT OFF YOUR BUCKET LIST

RATE THIS ACTIVITY

☆☆☆☆☆

THIS WOULD BE PERFECT FOR US BECAUSE...

MAKE IT HAPPEN: HOW? WHEN?

REVIEW
DATE COMPLETED: / /

WHAT HAPPENED? (PEOPLE MET, HIGH POINTS, CHALLENGES, EXPECTATIONS VS REALITY)

THE BEST PART WAS...

BUDGET

$

ANTICIPATED DATE

/ /   TO   / /

ACTION LIST

- ⊘
- ⊘
- ⊘
- ⊘
- ⊘
- ⊘
- ⊘
- ⊘
- ⊘

SUCCESS!

PLACE A CHECK HERE TO
TAKE IT OFF YOUR BUCKET LIST

RATE THIS ACTIVITY

☆☆☆☆☆

THIS WOULD BE PERFECT FOR US BECAUSE...

_____
_____
_____
_____

MAKE IT HAPPEN: HOW? WHEN?

_____
_____
_____
_____
_____

REVIEW

DATE COMPLETED: / /

WHAT HAPPENED? (PEOPLE MET, HIGH POINTS, CHALLENGES, EXPECTATIONS VS REALITY)

_____
_____
_____
_____

THE BEST PART WAS...

_____
_____
_____
_____
_____

BUDGET

$

ANTICIPATED DATE

/ /   TO   / /

ACTION LIST

- ⊘ _____
- ⊘ _____
- ⊘ _____
- ⊘ _____
- ⊘ _____
- ⊘ _____
- ⊘ _____
- ⊘ _____
- ⊘ _____

SUCCESS!

PLACE A CHECK HERE TO
TAKE IT OFF YOUR BUCKET LIST

RATE THIS ACTIVITY

☆☆☆☆☆

THIS WOULD BE PERFECT FOR US BECAUSE...

MAKE IT HAPPEN: HOW? WHEN?

REVIEW
DATE COMPLETED: / /

WHAT HAPPENED? (PEOPLE MET, HIGH POINTS, CHALLENGES, EXPECTATIONS VS REALITY)

THE BEST PART WAS...

BUDGET

$

ANTICIPATED DATE

/ /   TO   / /

ACTION LIST

⊘
⊘
⊘
⊘
⊘
⊘
⊘
⊘
⊘

SUCCESS!

PLACE A CHECK HERE TO
TAKE IT OFF YOUR BUCKET LIST

RATE THIS ACTIVITY

☆☆☆☆☆

THIS WOULD BE PERFECT FOR US BECAUSE...

_____

_____

_____

_____

MAKE IT HAPPEN: HOW? WHEN?

_____

_____

_____

_____

REVIEW

DATE COMPLETED: / /

WHAT HAPPENED? (PEOPLE MET, HIGH POINTS, CHALLENGES, EXPECTATIONS VS REALITY)

_____

_____

_____

_____

_____

THE BEST PART WAS...

_____

_____

_____

_____

BUDGET

$

ANTICIPATED DATE

/ /   TO   / /

ACTION LIST

⊘ _____
⊘ _____
⊘ _____
⊘ _____
⊘ _____
⊘ _____
⊘ _____
⊘ _____
⊘ _____

SUCCESS!

PLACE A CHECK HERE TO
TAKE IT OFF YOUR BUCKET LIST

RATE THIS ACTIVITY

☆☆☆☆☆

THIS WOULD BE PERFECT FOR US BECAUSE...

BUDGET

$

ANTICIPATED DATE

/ /   TO   / /

MAKE IT HAPPEN: HOW? WHEN?

ACTION LIST

⊘ _____
⊘ _____
⊘ _____
⊘ _____
⊘ _____
⊘ _____
⊘ _____
⊘ _____
⊘ _____

REVIEW

DATE COMPLETED: / /

WHAT HAPPENED? (PEOPLE MET, HIGH POINTS, CHALLENGES, EXPECTATIONS VS REALITY)

SUCCESS!

PLACE A CHECK HERE TO
TAKE IT OFF YOUR BUCKET LIST

THE BEST PART WAS...

RATE THIS ACTIVITY

☆☆☆☆☆

THIS WOULD BE PERFECT FOR US BECAUSE...

_____

_____

_____

MAKE IT HAPPEN: HOW? WHEN?

_____

_____

_____

_____

REVIEW

DATE COMPLETED: / /

WHAT HAPPENED? (PEOPLE MET, HIGH POINTS, CHALLENGES, EXPECTATIONS VS REALITY)

_____

_____

_____

_____

THE BEST PART WAS...

_____

_____

_____

_____

BUDGET

$

ANTICIPATED DATE

/ /   TO   / /

ACTION LIST

⊘ _____
⊘ _____
⊘ _____
⊘ _____
⊘ _____
⊘ _____
⊘ _____
⊘ _____
⊘ _____

(SUCCESS!)

PLACE A CHECK HERE TO
TAKE IT OFF YOUR BUCKET LIST

RATE THIS ACTIVITY

☆☆☆☆☆

THIS WOULD BE PERFECT FOR US BECAUSE...

MAKE IT HAPPEN: HOW? WHEN?

REVIEW
DATE COMPLETED: / /

WHAT HAPPENED? (PEOPLE MET, HIGH POINTS, CHALLENGES, EXPECTATIONS VS REALITY)

THE BEST PART WAS...

BUDGET

$

ANTICIPATED DATE

/ /   TO   / /

ACTION LIST

⊘
⊘
⊘
⊘
⊘
⊘
⊘
⊘
⊘

SUCCESS!

PLACE A CHECK HERE TO
TAKE IT OFF YOUR BUCKET LIST

RATE THIS ACTIVITY

☆☆☆☆☆

I HAVE LEARNED OVER THE YEARS THAT WHEN ONE'S MIND IS MADE UP, THIS DIMINISHES FEAR. — ROSA PARKS

THIS WOULD BE PERFECT FOR US BECAUSE...

_____

_____

_____

_____

MAKE IT HAPPEN: HOW? WHEN?

_____

_____

_____

_____

_____

REVIEW

DATE COMPLETED: / /

_____

WHAT HAPPENED? (PEOPLE MET, HIGH POINTS, CHALLENGES, EXPECTATIONS VS REALITY)

_____

_____

_____

_____

THE BEST PART WAS...

_____

_____

_____

_____

BUDGET

$

ANTICIPATED DATE

/ /   TO   / /

ACTION LIST

⊘ _____
⊘ _____
⊘ _____
⊘ _____
⊘ _____
⊘ _____
⊘ _____
⊘ _____
⊘ _____

SUCCESS!

PLACE A CHECK HERE TO
TAKE IT OFF YOUR BUCKET LIST

RATE THIS ACTIVITY

☆☆☆☆☆

IT DOES NOT MATTER HOW SLOWLY YOU GO AS LONG AS YOU DO NOT STOP. -- CONFUCIUS

THIS WOULD BE PERFECT FOR US BECAUSE...

_____

_____

_____

_____

MAKE IT HAPPEN: HOW? WHEN?

_____

_____

_____

_____

_____

_____

REVIEW

DATE COMPLETED: / /

WHAT HAPPENED? (PEOPLE MET, HIGH POINTS, CHALLENGES, EXPECTATIONS VS REALITY)

_____

_____

_____

_____

THE BEST PART WAS...

_____

_____

_____

_____

BUDGET

$

ANTICIPATED DATE

/ /   TO   / /

ACTION LIST

⊘ _____

⊘ _____

⊘ _____

⊘ _____

⊘ _____

⊘ _____

⊘ _____

⊘ _____

⊘ _____

SUCCESS!

PLACE A CHECK HERE TO
TAKE IT OFF YOUR BUCKET LIST

RATE THIS ACTIVITY

☆☆☆☆☆

THIS WOULD BE PERFECT FOR US BECAUSE...

_____

_____

_____

MAKE IT HAPPEN: HOW? WHEN?

_____

_____

_____

_____

REVIEW

DATE COMPLETED: / /

WHAT HAPPENED? (PEOPLE MET, HIGH POINTS, CHALLENGES, EXPECTATIONS VS REALITY)

_____

_____

_____

_____

THE BEST PART WAS...

_____

_____

_____

_____

BUDGET

$

ANTICIPATED DATE

/ /   TO   / /

ACTION LIST

⊘ _____
⊘ _____
⊘ _____
⊘ _____
⊘ _____
⊘ _____
⊘ _____
⊘ _____
⊘ _____

SUCCESS!

PLACE A CHECK HERE TO
TAKE IT OFF YOUR BUCKET LIST

RATE THIS ACTIVITY

☆☆☆☆☆

REMEMBER THAT NOT GETTING WHAT YOU WANT IS SOMETIMES A WONDERFUL STROKE OF LUCK. — DALAI LAMA

THIS WOULD BE PERFECT FOR US BECAUSE...

MAKE IT HAPPEN: HOW? WHEN?

REVIEW

DATE COMPLETED: / /

WHAT HAPPENED? (PEOPLE MET, HIGH POINTS, CHALLENGES, EXPECTATIONS VS REALITY)

THE BEST PART WAS...

BUDGET

$

ANTICIPATED DATE

/ /   TO   / /

ACTION LIST

- ⊘
- ⊘
- ⊘
- ⊘
- ⊘
- ⊘
- ⊘
- ⊘
- ⊘

SUCCESS!

PLACE A CHECK HERE TO
TAKE IT OFF YOUR BUCKET LIST

RATE THIS ACTIVITY

☆☆☆☆☆

YOU CAN'T USE UP CREATIVITY... THE MORE YOU USE, THE MORE YOU HAVE. – MAYA ANGELOU

ITEM #83: _____

THIS WOULD BE PERFECT FOR US BECAUSE...

_____
_____
_____
_____

MAKE IT HAPPEN: HOW? WHEN?

_____
_____
_____
_____
_____
_____

REVIEW

DATE COMPLETED: / /

WHAT HAPPENED? (PEOPLE MET, HIGH POINTS, CHALLENGES, EXPECTATIONS VS REALITY)

_____
_____
_____
_____
_____

THE BEST PART WAS...

_____
_____
_____
_____

BUDGET

$

ANTICIPATED DATE

/ /   TO   / /

ACTION LIST

⊘ _____
⊘ _____
⊘ _____
⊘ _____
⊘ _____
⊘ _____
⊘ _____
⊘ _____
⊘ _____

SUCCESS!

PLACE A CHECK HERE TO
TAKE IT OFF YOUR BUCKET LIST

RATE THIS ACTIVITY

☆☆☆☆☆

DREAM BIG AND DARE TO FAIL. — NORMAN VAUGHAN

THIS WOULD BE PERFECT FOR US BECAUSE...

BUDGET

$

ANTICIPATED DATE

/ /   TO   / /

MAKE IT HAPPEN: HOW? WHEN?

ACTION LIST

⊘ _____
⊘ _____
⊘ _____
⊘ _____
⊘ _____
⊘ _____
⊘ _____
⊘ _____
⊘ _____

REVIEW
DATE COMPLETED: / /

WHAT HAPPENED? (PEOPLE MET, HIGH POINTS, CHALLENGES, EXPECTATIONS VS REALITY)

SUCCESS!

PLACE A CHECK HERE TO
TAKE IT OFF YOUR BUCKET LIST

THE BEST PART WAS...

RATE THIS ACTIVITY

☆☆☆☆☆

THIS WOULD BE PERFECT FOR US BECAUSE…

_____

_____

_____

_____

MAKE IT HAPPEN: HOW? WHEN?

_____

_____

_____

_____

_____

REVIEW

DATE COMPLETED: / /

WHAT HAPPENED? (PEOPLE MET, HIGH POINTS, CHALLENGES, EXPECTATIONS VS REALITY)

_____

_____

_____

_____

_____

THE BEST PART WAS…

_____

_____

_____

_____

_____

BUDGET

$

ANTICIPATED DATE

/ /   TO   / /

ACTION LIST

⊘ _____
⊘ _____
⊘ _____
⊘ _____
⊘ _____
⊘ _____
⊘ _____
⊘ _____
⊘ _____

(SUCCESS!)

PLACE A CHECK HERE TO
TAKE IT OFF YOUR BUCKET LIST

RATE THIS ACTIVITY

☆☆☆☆☆

THIS WOULD BE PERFECT FOR US BECAUSE...

_____

_____

_____

MAKE IT HAPPEN: HOW? WHEN?

_____

_____

_____

_____

REVIEW
DATE COMPLETED: / /

WHAT HAPPENED? (PEOPLE MET, HIGH POINTS, CHALLENGES, EXPECTATIONS VS REALITY)

_____

_____

_____

_____

THE BEST PART WAS...

_____

_____

_____

_____

BUDGET

$ _____

ANTICIPATED DATE

/ /   TO   / /

ACTION LIST

⊘ _____
⊘ _____
⊘ _____
⊘ _____
⊘ _____
⊘ _____
⊘ _____
⊘ _____
⊘ _____

SUCCESS!

PLACE A CHECK HERE TO
TAKE IT OFF YOUR BUCKET LIST

RATE THIS ACTIVITY

☆☆☆☆☆

IF YOU DO WHAT YOU'VE ALWAYS DONE, YOU'LL GET WHAT YOU'VE ALWAYS GOTTEN. — TONY ROBBINS

ITEM #87: _____

THIS WOULD BE PERFECT FOR US BECAUSE...

_____
_____
_____

MAKE IT HAPPEN: HOW? WHEN?

_____
_____
_____
_____
_____

REVIEW

DATE COMPLETED: / /

WHAT HAPPENED? (PEOPLE MET, HIGH POINTS, CHALLENGES, EXPECTATIONS VS REALITY)

_____
_____
_____
_____

THE BEST PART WAS...

_____
_____
_____
_____

BUDGET

$

ANTICIPATED DATE

/ /   TO   / /

ACTION LIST

⊘ _____
⊘ _____
⊘ _____
⊘ _____
⊘ _____
⊘ _____
⊘ _____
⊘ _____
⊘ _____

SUCCESS!

PLACE A CHECK HERE TO
TAKE IT OFF YOUR BUCKET LIST

RATE THIS ACTIVITY

☆☆☆☆☆

DREAMING, AFTER ALL, IS A FORM OF PLANNING. — GLORIA STEINEM

THIS WOULD BE PERFECT FOR US BECAUSE...

MAKE IT HAPPEN: HOW? WHEN?

REVIEW

DATE COMPLETED: / /

WHAT HAPPENED? (PEOPLE MET, HIGH POINTS, CHALLENGES, EXPECTATIONS VS REALITY)

THE BEST PART WAS...

BUDGET

$

ANTICIPATED DATE

/ /   TO   / /

ACTION LIST

⊘ _____
⊘ _____
⊘ _____
⊘ _____
⊘ _____
⊘ _____
⊘ _____
⊘ _____
⊘ _____

SUCCESS!

PLACE A CHECK HERE TO
TAKE IT OFF YOUR BUCKET LIST

RATE THIS ACTIVITY

☆☆☆☆☆

PRIORITY ☆☆☆☆☆   ITEM #89: _____

THIS WOULD BE PERFECT FOR US BECAUSE...

_____

_____

_____

_____

MAKE IT HAPPEN: HOW? WHEN?

_____

_____

_____

_____

_____

REVIEW

DATE COMPLETED: / /

WHAT HAPPENED? (PEOPLE MET, HIGH POINTS, CHALLENGES, EXPECTATIONS VS REALITY)

_____

_____

_____

_____

THE BEST PART WAS...

_____

_____

_____

_____

_____

BUDGET

$

ANTICIPATED DATE

/ /   TO   / /

ACTION LIST

⊘ _____
⊘ _____
⊘ _____
⊘ _____
⊘ _____
⊘ _____
⊘ _____
⊘ _____
⊘ _____

SUCCESS!

PLACE A CHECK HERE TO
TAKE IT OFF YOUR BUCKET LIST

RATE THIS ACTIVITY

☆☆☆☆☆

THIS WOULD BE PERFECT FOR US BECAUSE...

_____
_____
_____

MAKE IT HAPPEN: HOW? WHEN?

_____
_____
_____
_____

REVIEW

DATE COMPLETED:　　/ /

WHAT HAPPENED? (PEOPLE MET, HIGH POINTS, CHALLENGES, EXPECTATIONS VS REALITY)

_____
_____
_____

THE BEST PART WAS...

_____
_____
_____
_____

BUDGET

$ _____

ANTICIPATED DATE

/ / TO / /

ACTION LIST

⊘ _____
⊘ _____
⊘ _____
⊘ _____
⊘ _____
⊘ _____
⊘ _____
⊘ _____
⊘ _____

SUCCESS!

PLACE A CHECK HERE TO
TAKE IT OFF YOUR BUCKET LIST

RATE THIS ACTIVITY

☆☆☆☆☆

ITEM #91: _____

THIS WOULD BE PERFECT FOR US BECAUSE...

_____
_____
_____
_____

MAKE IT HAPPEN: HOW? WHEN?

_____
_____
_____
_____
_____

REVIEW

DATE COMPLETED: / /

_____

WHAT HAPPENED? (PEOPLE MET, HIGH POINTS, CHALLENGES, EXPECTATIONS VS REALITY)

_____
_____
_____
_____
_____

THE BEST PART WAS...

_____
_____
_____
_____

BUDGET

$ _____

ANTICIPATED DATE

/ /   TO   / /

ACTION LIST

⊘ _____
⊘ _____
⊘ _____
⊘ _____
⊘ _____
⊘ _____
⊘ _____
⊘ _____
⊘ _____

SUCCESS!

PLACE A CHECK HERE TO
TAKE IT OFF YOUR BUCKET LIST

RATE THIS ACTIVITY

☆☆☆☆☆

THIS WOULD BE PERFECT FOR US BECAUSE...

_____

_____

_____

_____

MAKE IT HAPPEN: HOW? WHEN?

_____

_____

_____

_____

_____

REVIEW

DATE COMPLETED: / /

WHAT HAPPENED? (PEOPLE MET, HIGH POINTS, CHALLENGES, EXPECTATIONS VS REALITY)

_____

_____

_____

_____

THE BEST PART WAS...

_____

_____

_____

_____

_____

BUDGET

$

ANTICIPATED DATE

/ /   TO   / /

ACTION LIST

⊘ _____

⊘ _____

⊘ _____

⊘ _____

⊘ _____

⊘ _____

⊘ _____

⊘ _____

⊘ _____

SUCCESS!

PLACE A CHECK HERE TO
TAKE IT OFF YOUR BUCKET LIST

RATE THIS ACTIVITY

☆☆☆☆☆

THIS WOULD BE PERFECT FOR US BECAUSE...

_____
_____
_____
_____

MAKE IT HAPPEN: HOW? WHEN?

_____
_____
_____
_____
_____
_____

REVIEW

DATE COMPLETED: / /

_____

WHAT HAPPENED? (PEOPLE MET, HIGH POINTS, CHALLENGES, EXPECTATIONS VS REALITY)

_____
_____
_____
_____
_____

THE BEST PART WAS...

_____
_____
_____
_____

BUDGET

$

ANTICIPATED DATE

/ /   TO   / /

ACTION LIST

⊘ _____
⊘ _____
⊘ _____
⊘ _____
⊘ _____
⊘ _____
⊘ _____
⊘ _____
⊘ _____

(SUCCESS!)

PLACE A CHECK HERE TO
TAKE IT OFF YOUR BUCKET LIST

RATE THIS ACTIVITY

☆☆☆☆☆

THIS WOULD BE PERFECT FOR US BECAUSE...

_____

_____

_____

MAKE IT HAPPEN: HOW? WHEN?

_____

_____

_____

_____

REVIEW

DATE COMPLETED: / /

_____

WHAT HAPPENED? (PEOPLE MET, HIGH POINTS, CHALLENGES, EXPECTATIONS VS REALITY)

_____

_____

_____

_____

THE BEST PART WAS...

_____

_____

_____

_____

BUDGET

$

ANTICIPATED DATE

/ /   TO   / /

ACTION LIST

⊘ _____
⊘ _____
⊘ _____
⊘ _____
⊘ _____
⊘ _____
⊘ _____
⊘ _____
⊘ _____

SUCCESS!

PLACE A CHECK HERE TO
TAKE IT OFF YOUR BUCKET LIST

RATE THIS ACTIVITY

☆☆☆☆☆

IF YOU CAN DREAM IT, YOU CAN ACHIEVE IT. — ZIG ZIGLAR

ITEM #95: _____

THIS WOULD BE PERFECT FOR US BECAUSE...

_____

_____

_____

MAKE IT HAPPEN: HOW? WHEN?

_____

_____

_____

_____

REVIEW

DATE COMPLETED: / /

WHAT HAPPENED? (PEOPLE MET, HIGH POINTS, CHALLENGES, EXPECTATIONS VS REALITY)

_____

_____

_____

_____

_____

THE BEST PART WAS...

_____

_____

_____

_____

BUDGET

$

ANTICIPATED DATE

/ /   TO   / /

ACTION LIST

⊘ _____
⊘ _____
⊘ _____
⊘ _____
⊘ _____
⊘ _____
⊘ _____
⊘ _____
⊘ _____

SUCCESS!

PLACE A CHECK HERE TO
TAKE IT OFF YOUR BUCKET LIST

RATE THIS ACTIVITY

☆☆☆☆☆

THIS WOULD BE PERFECT FOR US BECAUSE...

_____

_____

_____

_____

MAKE IT HAPPEN: HOW? WHEN?

_____

_____

_____

_____

REVIEW

DATE COMPLETED: / /

WHAT HAPPENED? (PEOPLE MET, HIGH POINTS, CHALLENGES, EXPECTATIONS VS REALITY)

_____

_____

_____

_____

THE BEST PART WAS...

_____

_____

_____

_____

_____

BUDGET

$ _____

ANTICIPATED DATE

/ /   TO   / /

ACTION LIST

⊘ _____
⊘ _____
⊘ _____
⊘ _____
⊘ _____
⊘ _____
⊘ _____
⊘ _____
⊘ _____

SUCCESS!

PLACE A CHECK HERE TO
TAKE IT OFF YOUR BUCKET LIST

RATE THIS ACTIVITY

☆☆☆☆☆

ITEM #97: _____

THIS WOULD BE PERFECT FOR US BECAUSE...

_____
_____
_____
_____

MAKE IT HAPPEN: HOW? WHEN?

_____
_____
_____
_____
_____

REVIEW

DATE COMPLETED: / /

_____

WHAT HAPPENED? (PEOPLE MET, HIGH POINTS, CHALLENGES, EXPECTATIONS VS REALITY)

_____
_____
_____
_____
_____

THE BEST PART WAS...

_____
_____
_____
_____
_____
_____

BUDGET

$ _____

ANTICIPATED DATE

/ /   TO   / /

ACTION LIST

- ⊘ _____
- ⊘ _____
- ⊘ _____
- ⊘ _____
- ⊘ _____
- ⊘ _____
- ⊘ _____
- ⊘ _____
- ⊘ _____

SUCCESS!

PLACE A CHECK HERE TO
TAKE IT OFF YOUR BUCKET LIST

RATE THIS ACTIVITY

☆☆☆☆☆

THIS WOULD BE PERFECT FOR US BECAUSE...

MAKE IT HAPPEN: HOW? WHEN?

REVIEW

DATE COMPLETED: / /

WHAT HAPPENED? (PEOPLE MET, HIGH POINTS, CHALLENGES, EXPECTATIONS VS REALITY)

THE BEST PART WAS...

BUDGET

$

ANTICIPATED DATE

/ /   TO   / /

ACTION LIST

⊘
⊘
⊘
⊘
⊘
⊘
⊘
⊘
⊘

SUCCESS!

PLACE A CHECK HERE TO
TAKE IT OFF YOUR BUCKET LIST

RATE THIS ACTIVITY

☆☆☆☆☆

ONLY PUT OFF UNTIL TOMORROW WHAT YOU ARE WILLING TO DIE HAVING LEFT UNDONE. – PABLO PICASSO

PRIORITY ☆☆☆☆☆   ITEM #99: _____

THIS WOULD BE PERFECT FOR US BECAUSE...

_____

_____

_____

_____

MAKE IT HAPPEN: HOW? WHEN?

_____

_____

_____

_____

_____

REVIEW

DATE COMPLETED: / /

WHAT HAPPENED? (PEOPLE MET, HIGH POINTS, CHALLENGES, EXPECTATIONS VS REALITY)

_____

_____

_____

_____

_____

THE BEST PART WAS...

_____

_____

_____

_____

BUDGET

$

ANTICIPATED DATE

/ /   TO   / /

ACTION LIST

⊘ _____
⊘ _____
⊘ _____
⊘ _____
⊘ _____
⊘ _____
⊘ _____
⊘ _____
⊘ _____

SUCCESS!

PLACE A CHECK HERE TO
TAKE IT OFF YOUR BUCKET LIST

RATE THIS ACTIVITY

☆☆☆☆☆

AMATEURS SIT AND WAIT FOR INSPIRATION, THE REST OF US JUST GET UP AND GO TO WORK. – STEPHEN KING

THIS WOULD BE PERFECT FOR US BECAUSE...

_____

_____

_____

_____

MAKE IT HAPPEN: HOW? WHEN?

_____

_____

_____

_____

_____

REVIEW

DATE COMPLETED: / /

WHAT HAPPENED? (PEOPLE MET, HIGH POINTS, CHALLENGES, EXPECTATIONS VS REALITY)

_____

_____

_____

_____

THE BEST PART WAS...

_____

_____

_____

_____

_____

BUDGET

$

_____

ANTICIPATED DATE

/ /   TO   / /

_____

ACTION LIST

⊘ _____

⊘ _____

⊘ _____

⊘ _____

⊘ _____

⊘ _____

⊘ _____

⊘ _____

⊘ _____

SUCCESS!

PLACE A CHECK HERE TO
TAKE IT OFF YOUR BUCKET LIST

RATE THIS ACTIVITY

☆☆☆☆☆

THIS WOULD BE PERFECT FOR US BECAUSE...

_____

_____

_____

_____

MAKE IT HAPPEN: HOW? WHEN?

_____

_____

_____

_____

_____

_____

REVIEW
DATE COMPLETED: / /

WHAT HAPPENED? (PEOPLE MET, HIGH POINTS, CHALLENGES, EXPECTATIONS VS REALITY)

_____

_____

_____

_____

_____

THE BEST PART WAS...

_____

_____

_____

_____

_____

BUDGET

$

ANTICIPATED DATE

/ /   TO   / /

ACTION LIST

⊘ _____
⊘ _____
⊘ _____
⊘ _____
⊘ _____
⊘ _____
⊘ _____
⊘ _____
⊘ _____

SUCCESS!

PLACE A CHECK HERE TO
TAKE IT OFF YOUR BUCKET LIST

RATE THIS ACTIVITY

☆☆☆☆☆

© 2019 Superior Notebooks

Ordering Information
Order more copies of this title at
bit.ly/SuperiorNotebooks

Publisher's Cataloging-in-Publication data
Superior Notebooks.
Our Bucket List: An Anniversary Gift For Both Of Us.
Bucket List For Couples · Romantic Activity Planner
Journal / Superior Notebooks.
p. cm.

ISBN 9781090776112

1. Marriage. 2. Psychological recreations. 3.
Self-actualization (Psychology).--Examinations,
questions, etc. I. Superior Notebooks. II. Title.

Made in the USA
Las Vegas, NV
08 March 2021